Ganja

By Eric

*May your days be peaceful
and your nights be restful*

Thank You

To everyone who bought our first publication. Your support has made it possible to bring you this new revised, updated, re-tested and packed new book. We know you'll enjoy.

A big thank you to my friends and family and those with the difficult job of testing our recipes!

What fun we've had!

Contents

Thought

Keep your heroin poppy and seed
Give me your hash and a bundle of weed
I'll make us a cake
and a nice cup of tea
And you can come fly with me

Weights and Measures

Ounces	Grams	Pint	Millilitre	U.S
$1/32$	.75	$1/4$	142 ml	$2/3$ Cup
$1/16$	1.75	$1/2$	283 ml	$1/4$ Cup
$1/8$	3.5	$3/4$	425 ml	2 Cups
$1/4$	7	1 pint	567 ml	2 $1/2$ Cups
$1/2$	14	1 $1/2$	851 ml	3 $3/4$ Cups
1oz	28	1 $3/4$	992 (1 litre)	4 Cups
2oz	57			
3oz	85			
4 (1/4lb)	113			
5oz	142			
6oz	170			
7oz	198			
8 (1/2lb)	227			
16 (1lb)	450			

U.S. Measures

1lb Butter	= 2 Cups
1lb Flour	= 4 Cups
1lb Sugar	= 2 Cups
1lb Icing Sugar	= 3 Cups
8 oz Rice	= 1 Cup

Oven Temperatures

	C	F	Gas
Very cold	110	225	1/4
	120	250	1/2
Cool	140	275	1
	150	300	2
Moderate	160	325	3
	180	350	4
Mod. hot	190	375	5
	200	400	6
Hot	220	425	7
	230	450	8
Very hot	240	475	9

Terms Used

Hash	- plant resin in solid form
Buds	- strongest part of female plant
Leaves	- good for cooking with
Hash oil	- highly potent, thick liquid
Grass	- in its plant form
Ganja	- general term for all of the above

From the start

Cooking with Ganja first originated in 1994, from an old idea, many scribbled recipes and the continual requests of friends for our special recipes.

So, with my own bun in the oven I found the time to put together our first book. And we haven't looked back since, we daren't in case we fall over!

During this time we have met some great people and learnt a lot. There are many of you growing your own at home these days, with some really good results. A lot of plants produce large shade leaves. These are great for cooking with, you'll be surprised. So don't compost them, eat them!

About Ganja

P eople have been growing, smoking and eating Ganja in all parts of the world for many, many years. Therefore, it is grown in different climates which is why we have so many different strains, with a great variety of names.

Resin made from the plant is called Cannabis, hashish, hash, or pot. It comes in the forms of a light crumbly slate, or hard darker Morrocan to soft, oily black.

The hash and Ganja names usually depend on their country and village of origin. The plants being called Ganja, grass, herb, weed, marijuana, bhang, buds, bush. Some now have trade names for indoor growing. All are good for cooking with, as it can only improve the potency.

We have met a lot of you with a great need for more information on cooking with Ganja. As there are a lot of us who don't like to smoke. And some with illnesses which they find it helps.

It is well known that very small amounts of Ganja can help with migraine, depression, glaucoma, nausea relief, also for those with PMT's, and as a muscle relaxant. It can also help to aid sleep, relieve stress and help with eating problems. It is by no means the cure for all ills, but it can offer a little natural relief to some people.

As in our first book we have outlined a few important things to remember, so that you will always get the best from your ganja. The most important one being the THC (Tetrahydro-cannabinol) content, the bit that gets you stoned!

Freshly picked ganja is very acid in THC. This converts to non-acid THC when cooked and will increase the potency. However, over cooking will destroy the THC. Hash made from the best part of the plant, the buds and oils, is more concentrated and potent, and its effect lasts longer.

Potency however, will depend very much on the type of ganja used. By eating cooked ganja or hash, you will certainly become more stoned, and for a lot longer than you would from smoking the same amount. So don't eat too much too quickly as its effect can take anything from a half hour to an hour to start.

An empty stomach will speed things up a bit. Though be warned, have plenty of food in the house as we guarantee you'll get the munchies something bad!

Once you start eating other food, it will bring your feet back to the ground a bit, especially if you eat a meal afterwards.

THC is not soluble in water. It can be boiled to remove any acid taste, sometimes referred to as green. The water will not retain the THC. It is soluble only in fats, oils and alcohol by either soaking, boiling or sauté. It can also be combined with milk, which contains its own butter fats.

The effectiveness will be maintained if eaten in small amounts of food such as sweet or savoury biscuits, cakes or drinks. If eaten in a large curry it would get a bit lost. Due to public demand, we have our new savoury section and a dinner party menu for special days and friends. It comes with a warning: all guests should bring sleeping bags!

We have been collecting and adapting many recipes over the years, and we have found that the strong flavour of fresh ganja can be disguised very well by combining with other strong flavours. Chocolate and coffee, fresh herbs and spices and strong alcohols, like dark rum, brandy, red wine will serve only to improve the overall taste.

Sadly, our English law still looks upon this as a forbidden pastime. So be careful who eats your food, especially if they haven't eaten any before. Always let them know what they are eating so they can just try a little at first. Potency can be up to six times stronger than when smoked.

The buds of the female plant should be used more sparingly than the leaves. Hash (resin) will be a lot stronger too. The oils can be up to four times the strength of the hash they were made from.

Through the experience of cooking and eating, you will come to understand more about the many differences in strength and flavour and therefore, the amounts that suit you.

We have now stepped into the fast lane of life, and found the food processor is a wonderfully quick way to chop up those leaves to a fine powder with only a little grinding needed. Buds should be snipped off with a good pair of scissors.

Most recipes contain some sort of fat or oil. If you combine your Ganja with butter you will have made Cannabutter which can be used in your own favourite recipes.

In India a version of Cannabutter is known as Sacred Ghee. The Ghee being clarified butter, (all impurities removed). This butter will keep longer if you don't have a fridge. We have also found that many of the recipes within the book can be frozen successfully. This way you can make a larger amount and then defrost what is required later, instead of trying to get through 48 cakes between two of you, before they go stale!

Things you will need

A pestle and mortar (or a bowl and bottle)
Cooking scales
A fine sieve
A large poaching spoon
A small metal bowl (to heat hash in)
Cake tins (or see our tin-can cake)
A baking tray
Some grease-proof paper
Plus a few other odds and ends you're sure
to have in the kitchen
A food processor (if you have one)
And not forgetting the stash!

Basic Preparation

A guide to eating amounts

I have tried to give you a guide to how many people will get stoned with each recipe, but everyone has their own limits.

If you have not eaten Ganja before, then only small amounts should be taken. Even if you smoke a lot of Ganja, the effect when eaten will be more intense with a more trippy feel and the effect will last a lot longer than if the same amount is smoked.

If you should feel unwell – lay down in a quiet place and try to sleep it off. The worst thing that can happen to you is you will be sick. There is no record of anybody dying from eating Ganja, so don't panic.

$^1/_{16}$ oz (1.75 gms) Hash - 8 people mildly stoned
  - 4 people very stoned

$^1/_8$ oz (3.5 gms) Hash - 16 - 20 people mildly stoned
  - 8 - 10 people very stoned

$^1/_8$ oz Ganja buds - 8 - 10 people Stoned
  - 4 - 6 people very stoned

1 oz (28 gms) Ganja leaves - 20 people stoned
  - 10 people very stoned

1 gram Hash - 2 people very stoned

(small amounts are better in drinks)

Cannabutter

Ingredients

1lb (450g) butter

1 oz (28g) good ganja or hash

or

2 oz (57g) leaves

Method

Melt the butter slowly in a pan. Grind down your Ganja to a fine powder and sift out any stalky bits. Gently add to the melted butter and stir in well. It will turn dark green if you're using grass.

Keep on a low heat for up to half an hour without letting it burn whilst giving it plenty of stirring.

Then pour through a fine strainer squeezing all the butter into a jug. You can use the mush in a drink or simply compost it. Pour your Cannabutter into jars and seal them tightly for storage in the fridge. If you cover the hardened butter with a little water, this will help it keep a little longer.

Ounce weights

Butter	16 oz	8	4	2	1
Ganja	1 oz	$^1/_2$	$^1/_4$	$^1/_8$	$^1/_{16}$

Sacred Ghee

This will stop your butter from going rancid if you don't have a fridge. It will also have a nutty, butterscotch flavour.

Heat 1lb of butter slowly. Bring it to the boil and remove the froth from the top and discard it. Carry on until it stops frothing.

Your Ghee is now ready to add the Ganja using the same amounts as with Cannabutter.

If using Hash, firstly heat it in a bowl over a low heat. When it is warmed through it should crumble into a fine powder. Hash will dissolve quicker than grass so stir it into the Ghee on low heat for about 15 minutes, then strain and store as with Cannabutter.

Gram weights

Butter	450gms	227gms	113gms	57gms	28gms
Ganja	28gms	14gms	7gms	3.5gms	1.75gms

Cannabutter Using Water

If your Ganja is very acid in taste, this preparation will help overcome the bitterness.

Firstly, fill half of your pot with crushed Ganja and fill to 3/4 with water and melted butter or oil, using one part oil to four parts water.

Boil gently for 30 minutes. Stir as much as you can and using a poaching spoon remove any debris.

Allow the mixture to cool and then place pot in the fridge or freezer if you have used oil. When the butter has hardened on the top it can be removed, used or stored .

Bhang Paste

This is also a useful way to prepare your Ganja leaves, especially if you need a light fat content for a recipe.

4 oz (113g) ganja
10oz (300ml) water

Place Ganja in a pan of cold water and bring to the boil. Boil for five minutes then strain and remove any stalk or seed, then squeeze out any remaining water.

Then using a little milk, grind your Ganja in a pestle and mortar to form a thick paste ready for use.

Cooks Booze

Put $^1/_2$ oz of good buds or 1oz of leaves into a mason or kilner jar and cover with Rum or Brandy, and leave to soak for one week.

Then place the jar in a pan of shallow water, loosen the lid to allow the fumes to escape and heat gently for 30 minutes.

Strain the liquid while it is still hot. If you wish to add some hash, do it after straining. Pour the liquid back into the jar, add $^1/_4$ oz (7g) of good Ganja buds or $^1/_2$ oz (14g) of leaves, replace the lid and leave for another week.

Repeat this whole process another two times. Your liquid should now be dense with resin. Strain well and bottle in a clean wine bottle. Shake well before use.

Herb Butter

First prepare your Cannabutter and allow it to cool. Then take your fresh herbs and chop finely.

For every 2oz of Cannabutter use:

$1/2$ tbs of chives
$1/2$ tbs of parsley
$1/4$ tsp of tarragon
$1/2$ tsp of wholegrain mustard
salt/pepper

Method

Using a fork, blend the ingredients together and allow stand and cool before use.

If you like a garlic butter, add a crushed clove to your Cannabutter. It doesn't want to be too strong as it can be a bit overpowering with the flavour of Ganja.

Hash Oil Honey

Hash Oil comes in different refinements, from brown oil being its crudest, to red, amber, honey and white oil being the best.

Heat a tablespoon of Ghee or Butter for each gram of oil used. Then add to your oil and stir in well. Next add $1/2$ a cup of runny honey to each gram of oil used. Stir in over a low heat, pour into jars and allow to cool before putting the lids on.

One teaspoon should be sufficient for one person. It is nice on toast or in a cup of hot water for that good morning cup of hash oil tea.

Hash oil is about four times stronger than the hash it was made from. This means it is highly concentrated and it should be used with respect.

Sams' Sweet Things

On the following pages, you will find some of our all-time favourites and some great new ideas to suit all tastes. You'll find Ann's truffles a boon at parties and festivals. It is possible to make them on site with a double gas ring, two saucepan's, a bowl and a spoon. Also a cool box to keep your ingredients in and some greaseproof paper and tins to put them in. Though a box of truffles made at home beforehand is a lot easier!

Our Tin-Can cake is for anyone who hasn't a cake tin, and with our microwave magic it can all be done in seconds.

Mellow Browns

*From our original wild nut brownie recipe,
improved.*

Ingredients

> 6 oz (170g) butter
> 2 tbs cocoa
> 6 oz (170g) caster sugar
> 2 eggs
> 2 oz (57g) plain flour
> 2 oz (57g) chopped walnuts or pecan nuts
> 3 oz (85g) mini marshmallows
> 3 oz (85g) chocolate chips
> $^1/_8$ oz (3.5g) hash for 12 people
> > *or*
> $^1/_4$ oz (7g) buds for 12 people
> > *or*
> $^1/_2$ oz (14g) ground leaves

If you are using your Cannabutter, use 2oz of
Cannabutter and 4 oz of plain butter.

Method

Melt 2oz of the butter in a pan and add finely ground Ganja or crumbled Hash. Stir in well. Or simply melt 2oz of Cannabutter if you have made some.

Add the Cocoa and mix until smooth, set aside to cool. Cream together the remaining butter and sugar, beat in the eggs, add the cocoa mixture then fold in the walnuts and flour. Turn into a 7inch square greased baking tin and bake at 350 f or 180 c or gas mark 4 for 30 to 35 minutes.

Remove from the oven, sprinkle the marshmallows and chocolate chips evenly on the top and a few crushed nuts if you have them left. Return to the oven for 2 to 3 mins and allow to cool before cutting and place on a wire rack.

Ann's Truffles

Makes about 16 to 20 chocolates.
1 to 2 truffles each.

Ingredients

    1 oz (28g) butter
    1$\frac{1}{2}$ fluid oz (28ml) of rum
    4 oz (113g) chocolate
    4 oz (113g) icing sugar
    1 oz (28g) cocoa or vermicelli
    $\frac{1}{8}$ oz (3.5g) hash
        or
    $\frac{1}{4}$ oz (7g) good buds
        or
    $\frac{1}{2}$ to 1 oz (28g) leaves

For large amounts, around 350.

1lb butter
6 fluid oz (168ml) of rum
4lb chocolate
4lb icing sugar
$\frac{1}{2}$ lb vermicelli or cocoa
1 oz (28g) hash or good buds/4 oz (113g) leaves

Method

Melt the chocolate slowly in a bowl over a saucepan $1/4$ full of water or use a melting pan if you have one. In a separate saucepan , melt the butter and add ground ganja or crumbled hash (or melt down your ready made cannabutter). Then add rum and stir in. Next add the melted chocolate, stir in well and remove from the heat. Sift in the icing sugar and combine with a spoon until the mixture falls away from the sides of your pan.

Dust your hands with cocoa and roll the mixture into balls which should be soft and oily. Roll in vermicelli, place on greaseproof paper and pop in the fridge for a while if you can.

Instead of using rum we have found this is very successful with Whiskey, Chocolate Liqueur or Southern Comfort. The list is endless so why not try using your own favourite tipple.

Summer Ice Cream

Butterscotch flavour

We do find that hash is better in this recipe. The ice cream has a better colour and nicer flavour.
20 - 25 servings

Ingredients

2 tbs of butter
1 pint thin cream
3 oz (85g) sugar
pinch salt
3 oz (85g) bhang paste
or
$^1/_4$ oz (7g) hash finely crumbled

Method

Heat your cream slowly to near scalding. Heat the butter and sugar and salt adding your bhang or hash. Then add cream. Leave to cool then place in freezer in a suitable plastic tub. After 2 hours take out, beat well and put back for 1 hour. It is now ready for eating.

29

All in One Cake

This is a good easy sponge
For 8 - 10 people

Ingredients

6 oz (170g) plain flour
6 oz (170g) margarine
6 oz (170g) sugar
3 eggs
3 tsp baking powder
a drop of milk
$^1/_8$ (3.5g) oz hash
   or
$^1/_4$ oz (7g) good buds
   or
$^1/_2$ oz (14g) leaves

Method

Put the lot into processor and switch on for two minutes. Or put it all into a bowl and beat like mad. Then pour into 7 inch greased tin and bake for 25-30 minutes at 180c/350f/gas 4. Remove, allow to cool then turn out onto a wire rack.

You can also use the mixture to fill little paper cake cases for 24 to 30 individual cakes. If you don't have either of these, then clean out two opened tin cans, grease well and line with greaseproof paper, sticking out by about 1 inch. Divide mixture, fill just over half way and bake.

All sponges are tested for readiness by pressing the top, it should spring back and be golden brown. If you are not sure, spike it with a skewer, if it comes out clean, it is ready.

You can add 1 oz of cocoa and use only 5oz of flour for a chocolate sponge. Or you can use some grated lemon rind or juice of a lemon instead of milk for a lovely lemon sponge. Or add a teaspoon of instant coffee to 2-3 teaspoons of hot water and add instead of milk. Cover in cream or butter cream :-

> 4 oz (113g) butter
> 7 oz (198g) icing sugar
> 1-2 tbs of hot water.

Beat until light and creamy and cover cake.

Peanut Butter Cookies

Makes 20-25, about two each.

Ingredients

4 oz (113g) peanut butter
4 oz (113g) butter
$\frac{1}{2}$ tsp grated lemon rind
3 oz (85g) sugar
3 oz (85g) brown sugar
5 oz (142g) plain flour
1 tsp bicarbonate of soda
pinch salt
$\frac{1}{2}$ oz (14g) ground leaves
    or
$\frac{1}{4}$ oz (7g) good buds
    or
$\frac{1}{8}$ (3.5g) hash

Method

If using your ready made cannabutter, use 1oz to 3oz plain butter

Cream together butter, lemon rind, ganja, peanut butter, sugar (brown and white). Then sift in flour, soda, salt, fold into mixture and then roll into small balls. Dust your hands with flour or they will stick to you. Place on a greased oven sheet and press down with the back of a fork. Bake for 15 minutes on the middle shelf at about 180c/350f/gas4.

Allow to cool for a few minutes before removing onto a wire rack. Try to leave to cool before eating, that's the hardest part!

Chocolate Munchy Cake

for 10 – 12 people

Ingredients

    2 tbs fresh double cream
    4 oz (113g) plain chocolate
    4 oz (113g) butter
    $\frac{1}{2}$ egg
    4 oz (113g) digestive biscuits (lightly crushed)
    1 oz (28g) glace cherries (washed, chopped)
    2 oz (57g) flaked almonds
    $\frac{1}{8}$ oz (3.5g) hash
       or
    $\frac{1}{4}$ oz (7g) good buds
       or
    $\frac{1}{2}$ oz (14g) ground leaves

Method

Grease a loose based 7 inch flan tin or ring. Melt chocolate in a bowl over a pan a $\frac{1}{4}$ full of not quite boiling water. Melt the butter and add Ganja, or melt 1 oz Cannabutter with 3 oz of plain butter. Add the cream and mix well. Allow to cool. Beat the egg lightly and stir into cream mix, then add all other ingredients. Smooth off and chill for 1 hour before eating.

Chocolate Orange Truffles

Makes 15 – 20 depending on size
1 – 2 each

Ingredients

4 oz (113g) plain chocolate
2 oz (57g) butter
2 egg yolks
grated zest of $^1/_2$ an orange
1 tbs of orange juice or rum
3 oz (85g) ground almonds
2 oz (57g) grated chocolate
1 oz (28g) cocoa
$^1/_8$ oz (3.5g) hash (finely crumbled)
   or
$^1/_4$ oz (7g) good ganja
   or
$^1/_2$ oz (14g) ground leaves

Method

Melt chocolate in a bowl over a pan a $^1/_4$ full of not quite boiling water. Melt the butter and add the Ganja or melt 1 oz Cannabutter with 1 oz plain butter. Remove from the heat, add egg yolks, orange zest, orange juice or rum and the almonds. Add the grated chocolate to form a thick paste and leave to go cold. Roll into balls, dust in cocoa to serve.

Creamy Hash Fudge

Makes ¹/₂ lb – for 30 people

Ingredients

> 4 oz (113g) butter
> 1 x 15 oz tin of condensed milk
> 1 lb (450g) castor sugar
> ¹/₄ oz (7g) hash
>   *or*
> ¹/₂ oz (14g) buds

Method

Line an 8 inch square tin with greaseproof paper. Melt the butter slowly in a pan slowly adding the Ganja. Add the milk and sugar stirring continuously until all the sugar has dissolved. (A heavy based pan is best, or the mixture tends to burn.) This is the hardest bit... Still stirring, raise the heat and let the mixture boil! Don't stop stirring! The mixture is ready when it starts to fall away from the sides of the pan. Pour into a prepared tray and allow to cool at room temperature. Before it completely firms off mark into 1 inch squares.

It's worth the aching arm!

Or try our fast fudge on page 63.

Solstice Celebration Cake

*This is a must for your Solstice Celebration and
it's well worth the time and effort.*
20 people totally smashed
(It's best made about six weeks before eating)

Ingredients

6 oz (170g) madeira or sherry or Cooks Booze
(page 19)

2 oz (57g) apricots (chopped, washed)

6 oz (170g) mixed coloured glace cherries (chopped,
washed)

2 oz (57g) chopped Brazil nuts

4 oz (113g) mixed peel (washed)

2 oz (57g) crystallised ginger (chopped, washed)

2 oz (57g) ground almonds

2 oz (57g) glace pineapple (chopped, washed)

12 oz (340g) plain flour

9 oz (255g) butter

2 tsp baking powder

9 oz (255g) caster sugar

4 eggs (beaten)

1 lb (450g) jar of apricot jam

grated rind of a lemon

3 oz (85g) mixed fruit and nuts for decoration

1 oz (28g) ground leaves

(if using Cooks Booze, use $\frac{1}{2}$ oz (14g)

and

$\frac{1}{2}$ oz (14g) buds

and

$\frac{1}{4}$ (7g) or $\frac{1}{8}$ oz (3.5g) hash

37

Method

DAY ONE

Put Sherry or Madeira (3 oz / 85g) into a pan to warm through. Crumble in the fine hash, stir well and keep on a low heat for about 15 minutes. Then pour the mixture over the washed and chopped fruit and leave over night.

Then make your Cannabutter using 3 oz / 85g butter with 1 1/2 oz (42g) grass and leave to go hard over night.

DAY TWO

Grease an 8 inch cake tin and line with Greaseproof paper. Heat oven to 160c, 325f, gas 3.

Sift the flour and baking powder into a bowl. Set aside. Then add to yesterday's fruit mixture; the brazil nuts, ground almonds, lemon rind and a few spoons of the flour mix. In another bowl, cream together the Cannabutter, 6 oz / 170g of plain butter and the sugar until light and fluffy. Add your beaten eggs gradually with a spoon full of flour after each egg. Then stirring well, add the remaining flour.

Next, add to this the fruit mixture and another 2 oz / 57g of the Madeira so the mixture is just pourable. Turn this into a tin and bake for 1 1/2 hours. Then turn the oven down to 150c, 300f, gas 2 and continue to bake for a further 1 1/2 to 2 hours.

Test the cake with a clean skewer by gently inserting it into the centre of the cake. If it appears clean then remove the cake and allow to cool for ten minutes before turning out onto a wire rack. When the cake is cold, make small holes in the top and bottom and pour a little of the remaining Madeira or Sherry over the cake regularly. (About once a week.)

This cake will keep for up to 6 weeks if wrapped in foil and kept in a tin. It stays moist and becomes very potent if this is done, so it's well worth the effort.

To decorate your cake, wait until it is to be eaten. Heat the jam slowly and spread a thin layer over the whole cake. Then cover with a pattern of fruit and nuts of your choice. Make sure your guests have somewhere to crash out as they won't go far after this!

Happy Solstice!

Chocolate Ganja Cake

Great for Birthdays
For 6 – 8 people

Ingredients

4 oz (113g) butter
4 oz (113g) sugar
2 tbs of golden syrup
1 Egg
1 drop of vanilla extract
6 oz (170g) plain flour
2 tbs cocoa
$^1/_4$ tsp salt
1 tsp baking powder
$^1/_2$ cup of milk

1 tsp bicarbonate of soda
$^1/_4$ oz (7g) good buds
    or
$^1/_8$ oz (3.5g) hash
    or
$^1/_2$ oz (14g) ground leaves

(Black Hash is especially good)

Method

Melt the butter and add the Ganja stirring in well. (Or melt 2 oz Cannabutter and 2 oz plain butter.) Then add the sugar and syrup stirring in well and remove from the heat.

In a separate bowl, mix together; the flour, cocoa, salt and baking powder. Then beat the eggs until thick and add to your pan of Cannabutter mixture. Then add $1/2$ of the dry ingredients mix and the vanilla extract.

Next stir the bicarbonate of soda into the milk and add this this to the final mix with the rest of the dry ingredients. Stir well.

Pour the mixture into a greased and lined 7 inch cake tin and bake for 30 – 40 minutes on the middle shelf at 190c, 375f, gas 5.

Test the cake with a clean skewer by gently inserting it into the centre of the cake. If it appears clean then remove and allow to cool for ten minutes before turning out onto a wire rack to cool completely. Cover in whipped cream or buttercream and serve. It won't make you any younger but you'll have a good birthday!

Drinks Bit

Hash Bhang

For Two People

Ingredients

$1/8$ oz (3.5g) butter
2 cups of milk
1 – 2 grams of hash
a pinch of spice

Method

Melt the butter in a pan with crumbled hash and simmer for one minute. Then add the milk and warm through gently. Strain and pour into cups. You may like to add a little honey or sugar and a pinch of spices. Cinnamon is nice, or if you are feeling extravagant, squirt cream on top and sprinkle with the bits caught in the strainer with a dash of cocoa.

Bhang Bhang

For 8 – 10 People

Ingredients

$^1/_8$ oz (3.5g) finely ground buds
$^1/_8$ oz (3.5g) butter
8 fl oz (250ml) Vodka
A dash of spice

Method

Melt the butter and stir in the Ganja while it is sizzling.
Then add the Vodka and simmer gently for one minute.
Add your chosen spice and strain, discarding the mush.
Add honey or sugar to taste.

This has a kick to it!

We have also found a little coconut milk added gives a
good taste.

Two for Tea

THC is not soluble in water, so steeping the leaves to make tea only produces flavour. A teaspoon of Hash oil honey will work when added to boiling water.

Alternatively, you can use some Vodka. Heat slowly and crumble in your hash. stir well until it has dissolved and add to regular tea.

1 gram of Hash to 1 oz Alcohol.

You can also add the hot mixture to a bottle of wine. Remove the equivalent amount of wine from the bottle, introduce the hot Vodka mixture and re-cork the bottle. Shake well but remember your wine will be more alcoholic with the Vodka added.

Sleepy Chocolate

For two people

Fill two cups with milk, pour into a pan and warm through. Add 1-2 grams of finely crumbled hash and heat gently but do not let it boil.

Then pour back into the cups and add a teaspoon of drinking chocolate or cocoa to each cup. Add sugar if required and squirt with cream or sprinkle with grated chocolate for real luxury. *Sleep well!*

Can also be made with coffee instead of cocoa.

Fruity Wine

Ingredients

    1 oz (28g) ground ganja leaves
    1 pint of mild beer
    2 lb (900g) sugar
    4 fresh fruits (either peaches, pears or nectarines)
    A large Kilner jar or container with a tight lid.

Method

Stab the fruit all over, place into the jar, pour on the beer and stir in the Ganja with the sugar. Leave for 6 weeks stirring every day. Be sure to re-seal the lid each time. After 6 weeks, strain through a muslin cloth and bottle. This makes a very sweet liqueur type wine.

Black Coffee

For four people

1 tbs brown sugar	A strip of orange peel
$1/16$ (1.75g) finely ground hash	A strip of lemon peel
5 cloves	$1/2$ cinnamon stick
	$1/2$ a vanilla pod
	$1/4$ pint of brandy

Place all the ingredients in a pan and heat gently until all the sugar has dissolved. Ignite with a match and let it flare over for 15 seconds and then cover with a lid. Pour into cups that are 3/4 full of hot, black coffee and serve.

48

Savoury Style

Mama's Sauce

A good sauce for your favourite pasta dishes.
for 6 people

Ingredients

1 onion (peeled & chopped)
1 celery stick (chopped)
1 carrot (chopped)
4 mushrooms (chopped)
2 tbs olive oil
1 clove garlic (crushed)
14 oz (400g) tin tomatoes
$^1/_2$ tsp basil
$^1/_2$ tsp oregano
5 fl oz stock or red wine
salt & pepper
1 oz (28g) ground ganja leaves

Method

Gently fry onions, celery and carrot for ten minutes. Then add the Ganja, Garlic, tomatoes, mushrooms, herbs and wine and simmer gently for 20 minutes giving it a good stir. Remove from the heat and then season. If it is too thick, add a little more stock or some wine.

This sauce freezes well.

Veggie Burgers

For 6 – 8 people

Ingredients

4 oz (113g) chopped nuts
4 oz (113g) breadcrumbs
4 oz (113g) cooked cauliflower
4 oz (113g) cooked carrots
2 medium sized cooked potatoes
1 tbs parsley (chopped)
$^{1}/_{2}$ grated onion
1 egg
salt & pepper
2 oz (57g) cannabutter
1 cup plain flour

Method

Mash all the vegetables with butter and add all the other ingredients. Shape into burgers, then roll in the flour and fry until golden brown. A slice of cheese melting on top is nice!

Fetta Parcels

For 6 – 8 people

Ingredients

1 large onion (chopped)
1 $\frac{1}{2}$ lb of frozen chopped spinach (defrosted and drained)
8 oz (227g) fetta cheese
2 bunches of spring onions (chopped)
1 oz (28g) parsley (chopped)
salt & pepper
10 sheets of filo pastry (or you can use a block of defrosted puff pastry)
$\frac{1}{2}$ (14g) ground leaves *or* $\frac{1}{8}$ oz (3.5g) buds *or* hash

Method

Melt 1 oz butter and fry the onions for five minutes. Add the Ganja and stir in well keeping it on a low heat for a few minutes. Meanwhile, put the spinach in a bowl, crumble over with cheese, add the onions, herbs, and eggs. Mix well.

Lay the pastry on a flat surface , melt the remaining butter and brush it on the inside. Add a little of the mixture and fold the pastry over to make a parcel. Score with a knife and bake for 25 – 30 minutes at 180f, 350c, gas 4. If using puff pastry, roll out and cut into squares and repeat the process.

Green Straws

Makes about 40
5 – 10 each

Ingredients

2 oz (57g) plain flour
1 ¹/₂ oz (42g) butter
1 ¹/₂ oz (42g) finely grated cheese
salt & pepper (Cayenne pepper is good)
1 egg yolk or milk
¹/₄ oz (7g) ground leaves
   or
¹/₈ oz (3.5g) ground buds
   or
¹/₁₆ (1.75g) oz hash

Method

Rub the butter into the flour and add the cheese, seasoning and Ganja. Add a little of the egg yolk or milk to bring the mixture to a firm dough. Knead a little and make into straws or any other shape of your choice. Bake for 10 – 12 minutes at 230c, 450f, gas 7.

you can double the recipe for enough pastry to make a flan, though it is better to keep the Ganja amount the same as it tends to become too green.

This dough freezes well.

Asparigrass Soup

For 6 – 8 people

Ingredients

2 oz (57g) Cannabutter
1 oz (28g) flour
1 small onion
A little cream
1 ¹/₂ lb (680g) asparagus
1 ¹/₂ (851ml) pints water or stock
salt and pepper

Method

Use your ready prepared cannabutter (p16). Heat gently and fry finely chopped onion until soft. Blend in the flour and stock or water and bring to the boil. Add chopped asparagus and simmer gently until tips are very soft - about 20-25 mins. Then rub the mixture through a sieve or put in a blender if you have one. When smooth, return to pan, stir in cream, salt and pepper. Nice served with a crusty roll and butter.

Ganja Crisps

Makes 25, 2-3 each

Ingredients

4 oz (113g) unsalted butter
4 oz (113g) Stilton cheese crumbled
2 oz (57g) blanched, chopped almonds
4 oz (113g) plain flour
4 drops tobasco sauce
1 egg
1 oz (28g) poppy seeds
$^{1}/_{2}$ oz (14g) ground leaves
  or
$^{1}/_{4}$ oz (7g) ground buds
  or
$^{1}/_{8}$ oz (3.5g) hash

Method

Beat butter and cheese together until creamy, add finely ground ganja and mix in well. Add the almonds, flour, $^{1}/_{2}$ egg, and tobasco sauce, beat until smooth. Roll into a log shape about 1 $^{1}/_{2}$ inches in diameter and wrap in cling film. Leave in fridge for 1 hour then cut into thin slices and place on a lightly greased baking tray. Brush with the other half of beaten egg, sprinkle with poppy seeds and bake 15 mins at 200c, 400f, gas 6 until crisp and golden. *Freezes well.*

Pizza Mary Jane

For 8 – 10 people

Ingredients

2 pizza bases
1 small jar tomato pizza sauce
$^1/_2$ red pepper
4 oz (113g) sliced mushroom
$^1/_2$ onion chopped
8 oz (227g) grated cheese
Green or black olives
olive oil
$^1/_2$ oz (14g) ground leaves
   or
$^1/_4$ oz (7g) ground buds
or
$^1/_8$ oz (3.5g) hash

Method

Gently fry onion and pepper in oil until soft, add ganja and mushrooms and cook gently for a few minutes. Spread bases with tomato pizza sauce, divide your mixture between pizzas, grate over cheese, sprinkle mixed herbs if you like then bake under a hot grill or in oven for 10 minutes.

For the Vegan

There are many substitutes for most of the dairy products used in this book. Here are some:

Agar Agar - from seaweed. Can be used as a gelatin.

Carob - instead of chocolate

Soya milk, cream, yogurt, are all available.

Tahini - mixed with maple syrup makes a nice cream substitute.

And there are a variety of **margarines** that can be used in the same way as butter.

Soya flour can be used as an alternative to egg and so can oil as in the following recipe.

Vegan Sponge Cake

Ingredients

10 oz (275g) self raising flour
2 oz (57g) cocoa
3 tsp baking powder
9oz (255g) castor sugar
9tbs sunflower oil
12 fl oz (320ml) water
vegan margarine for greasing
1 tsp vanilla extract
$^{1}/_{4}$ oz (7g) good buds

or

$^{1}/_{8}$ oz (3.5g) hash

or

$^{1}/_{2}$ oz (14g) ground leaves

For the topping

4 oz (113g) vegan margarine
7 oz (198g) icing sugar
cocoa
1-2 tbs hot water

Method

Grease two 8 inch sandwich tins and line with grease-proof paper. Heat oven to 170c, 325f, gas 3.

Sift the flour, cocoa and baking powder into a bowl. Add the sugar, vanilla, oil, water and your ganja and mix well to a batter-like consistency. Pour into tins and bake for 35 to 40 mins. When the cakes are firm to the touch, remove from the oven, leave to cool, then turn out onto a wire rack. For the topping, cream together the margarine and sugar with a little hot water and the cocoa, and spread over the cake.

Or if you have a spare leaf, place it on the cake and sift over with icing sugar until the cake is covered. Carefully remove the leaf for an impressive effect.

For a lemon flavoured cake, follow directions as above, replacing the 2oz / 57g of cocoa in the cake mix with 2oz / 57g self raising flour, and replace 2 tbs of the water with 2tbs of lemon juice and grated rind. For the topping, replace cocoa with lemon juice.

Microwave Magic

This is for all those who have a microwave and for those who want instant food munchies! We have had great fun experimenting with our microwave, and we hope you'll enjoy these ideas. We cannot guarantee things won't suddenly explode, but you can be sure you'll enjoy the food. We are not scientists but as far as we can tell, the microwave does not effect the potency of Ganja within the food so long as it is not over-cooked. We have found it's better to cook in smaller amounts, as the food will burn quickly. When cooking stay within reach of your microwave at all times!

Recipes containing a lot of sugar should be cooked in a glass or pottery bowl as plastic containers may melt or distort with the heat. The cooking times vary from one microwave to another depending on the wattage. It is also important to let food stand and cool down and to check it regularly while it is cooling. If you have some ganja leaves, these are good for your first attempts, until you are confident of the exact cooking times for your machine. Do this before you start on your best buds.

We found the flavour of the ganja a little bit stronger when using a microwave, especially with grass.

Flat on Your Back Jack!

For 8 to 10 people

Ingredients

8 oz (227g) porridge oats
4 oz (113g) butter
3 oz (85g) soft brown sugar
3 tbs golden syrup
1 oz (28g) nuts (chopped)
2 oz (57g) dried fruit
pinch salt
1tsp baking powder
$^1/_2$ oz (14g) ground leaves
    or
$^1/_4$ oz (7g) good buds
    or
$^1/_8$ oz (3.5g) crumbled hash

Method

Melt the sugar and butter together in a glass bowl, add the ganja and heat for 30 seconds. Stir in the syrup, salt, baking powder, oats, fruit and nuts and mix well. Turn into a buttered, shallow microwave dish, or two smaller ones, pat flat with the back of a spoon. Cook on a high setting for five minutes. Check occasionally to see that it does not burn in the middle. When done, leave to rest for 15 minutes before cutting into squares for eating.

Magic Castles

Makes 6, 1 each

Ingredients

4 $^1/_2$ oz (127g) self raising flour
3 oz (85g) butter
1 egg (beaten)
1 $^1/_2$ tbs milk
$^1/_2$ tsp baking powder
2 $^1/_2$ oz (71g) soft brown sugar
3/4 can of fruit pie filling
6 paper drinking cups (not plastic)
$^1/_4$ oz (7g) ground buds or leaves
  or
$^1/_{16}$ oz (1.75g) crumbled hash

Method

Rub butter and flour together, add baking powder, sugar and ganja. Stir in well. Add the egg, milk and half the fruit filling. Put a tablespoon of the remaining fruit filling in each cup. Then fill each cup to half way with the mixture and cook on a high setting for three minutes, turning once. When the sponge is firm to the touch, remove and let them stand for a few minutes. Then tip the cups up onto a plate. These are nice with cream. The cups can be washed and reused several times.

Fast Fudge

Makes 40, 1-2 each

Ingredients

2 oz (57g) butter
2 tbs water
2 tbs golden syrup
1lb (450g) granulated sugar
8 tbs condensed milk
1 oz (28g) nuts (chopped)
$\frac{1}{8}$ oz (3.5g) crumbled hash
    or
$\frac{1}{2}$ oz (14g) ground leaves
    or
$\frac{1}{4}$ oz (7g) buds

Method

Put everything into a large, glass microwave bowl, and cook on a high setting for two minutes. Give it a good stirring, then cook for a further five to six minutes. When a little of the mixture is dropped in some cold water in a saucer, it should go hard. This is called the soft ball stage, be careful because the mixture is very hot. When it has reached this stage, pour into a greased, shallow dish and leave to cool. Cut into squares just before it sets firm. Any crumbs can be sprinkled over ice cream for a delicious topping!

Micro Cocoa

Take 4oz / 113g of good milk chocolate, break into pieces and place in a plastic microwave bowl. Place in the oven on full heat for half a minute, then remove and add $^1/_{16}$ oz / 1.75g of crumbled hash. stir this in and cook for a further half minute until the chocolate is well melted.

This recipe can be used to cover nuts such as pecans, brazil's or dried fruit. you can make up a nice box for a present or try making our peppermint creams.

Peppermint Creams

Beat one egg white until light and fluffy not stiff. Add 10oz / 284g icing sugar and a few drops of peppermint oil. Mix gradually until mixture becomes a stiff dough. Knead and roll out on an icing sugared surface. Cut out shapes as you want and dip into chocolate as above. Lay on a sheet of greaseproof paper to harden off.

Dinner Party Dreams

For four people

Starter
Grapefruit

You will need two grapefruits. Cut them in half and loosen the segments. Melt $^1/_2$ oz cannabutter with 1/2oz brown sugar, a drop of sherry and a pinch of mixed spice, stir over a low heat for a few minutes then pour over grapefruit and place under the grill for a further few minutes before serving.

Main Meal
Spring Flan

Ingredients

> 8 oz (227g) green straw pastry (p55)
> 5fl oz single cream or milk
> 2 eggs
> 1 tbs fresh herbs finely chopped
> 2 tbs fresh buds finely chopped
> salt and pepper
> 4 spring onions
> pinch of nutmeg

Heat oven to 190c, 375f, gas 5. Grease and line tin or flan ring with pastry and trim the edges with a knife.

Method

Whisk together cream or milk with eggs, herbs, ganja, nutmeg and salt and pepper. Chop onions and lay in dish, cover with cream mixture and bake on top shelf 35-40 minutes until filling has set. Serve with green salad and crusty bread.

Pudding

Sweet Bananas

Ingredients

4 bananas peeled, cut in half and lengthways
1 peach
Juice of $1/2$ lemon
1 tbs peach juice
2 fl oz of our fruity wine (page 47)
or use an alcohol of your choice
1 oz (28g) brown sugar
$1/2$ tsp cinnamon

Method

Lay bananas in an oven proof dish, sprinkle with sugar and cinnamon. Add juice and wine together and pour over bananas. Bake in the oven for 30 mins at 180c, 350f, gas 4. And serve with our butterscotch ice cream or plain cream

Party On!